oH mY fuCkINg gOd i WrOTe A boOK

of poems

Charmmare Daugherty

oH mY fuCkINg gOd i WrOTe A boOK

of poems

Charmmare Daugherty

oH mY fuCkINg gOd i WrOTe A boOK of poems
Copyright © 2026 by Charmmare Daugherty.

MILTON & HUGO L.L.C.
1001 3rd Avenue West,
Suite 430 Bradenton,
FL 34205, USA

Website: www. miltonandhugo.com
Hotline: 1- 888-778-0033
Email: info@miltonandhugo.com

Ordering Information:
Quantity sales. Special discounts are available on quantity purchases by corporations, associations, and others. For details, contact the publisher at the address above.

Library of Congress Control Number: 2026903433
ISBN-13:   979-8-89285-780-2 [Paperback Edition]
                       979-8-89285-781-9 [Hardback Edition]
                       979-8-89285-782-6 [Digital Edition]

Rev. date: 01/28/2026

Table of Contents

My, my, my do I have a story to tell...take a walk with me through my journey dealing with the abuse, neglect, and trauma inflicted on me, in the form of poems. I fell in love with poetry the moment it was introduced to me in elementary, finally finding an outlet to fully express how I truly felt without guilt or shame but with power and release. The rhyming thing also really got me hooked, for whatever reason it doesn't feel like a poem if it doesn't rhyme; plus I liked the challenge in finding the right rhyming word. The first few poems come from my first experience at The Brook, leading you through years of battles I'm still fighting today. In the midst of all this pain and gut wrenching moments, there was always a spark of hope, a knowing that I'm not doomed and my life isn't over. Something in me knew I could change, outgrow everything I knew, and actually become the person I want to be, you can too.

My Inner Self

Me and my inner self kinda don't get along
On the inside I could be right and
on the outside feel wrong
My physical body and my spirit just drifted apart
And it's like each side has half my heart
I'm so lost and confused and tired and can be
I don't know what to do how to find me
My inner self and I are on a different page
One minute I'm up then she takes the stage
I go back and forth, deciding what's right
But I'm tired of it, I'm done with this fight
I've tried so hard to connect with myself
But nothing I do really seems to help
I feel so hopeless like I'll never be whole
"Who are you?" they ask, I don't even know
I don't understand myself or the mood swings I have
I just hate the way I am, it makes me mad
So, until I find my true inner self, I'll be
lost in space, floating in hell

Scars

The scars on my body are here for a reason
It's because I'm hurt, broken down, and beaten
No, I don't do them to gain the attention
I do them with purpose and with intention
I don't want to die or end my life
I want my skin to burn with the blade of the knife
My reasons for doing this vary much so
The first is because of self-hate and there's more to go
The second is due to having no emotion
I'd still feel empty when I just felt commotion
The third for me provided a distraction
There was too much inside so I took action
The fourth and last, was due to my past, I
spent too long performing this task
I became so close I could overdose, I
was so addicted I just lost hope
But I know one day I'll be happy with no need to cut
I'll be a better person than I previously was

Flowers

There are more to flowers then the eye can meet
They are wonderful creatures, you
just have to take a peak
When you first look at a flower it's balled up, closed
Just like a person with secrets untold
When the flower opens up, you see what's inside
It's truly beautiful, just like a person that hides
Though it takes some time for the flower to bloom
You have to have patience and give it some room
Just like the people with struggles of opening up
You have to give them time and show them your love
After they are ready they finally come out
And is full of of color and life
Just like a person who's secrets come now
Their darkness turns into light
Like flowers we are gorgeous on the inside and out
Once we open up, we are heard, speak loud!

Death

Talking about death sent shivers down my spine
Just the thought would get me everytime
Now being here and living life the way i am
Getting death off my mind? I don't think I can
I've been in and out of therapy and the hospital too
I feel like I've tried everything I
don't know what else to do
I'm starting to give up I just want to die
They all say "no" but haven't traveled through my mind
They don't know what I go through from the inside out
Or the the fact that I have demons that break me down
I just wish they understood, I wish they could see
But they can't and they won't so I'm done with trying
They plan on "helping' while I plan on dying
I wanna slit my wrist and watch the blood flow
Then swallow too many pills until I finally go

Purgatory

Will I be like this in my 40's?
Still sad and sorry?
Wishing for glory without moving forward?

Stuck in my ways
I always cave

The unknown saves
But why do I stay?

Will I be like this in my 20's?
Only two years away, not counting the days
Time is weird in purgatory

Fade

I see you, I hear you, I feel you yet you fade
I care I swear, yet it still slips away
When you hurt me, you'll know I'm not straight
But when I hurt you I'm confused for days
I'm here, but I'm not, yet I don't try to be
I'm not scared of reality, I'm scared of me
I'm living, breathing, blinking, so what I know stays
Yet it still doesn't click, and everything just fades

Dance w/ the Devil

I put on that red dress
the one that we met in
I know in your presence
the best is expected
I've learned all my lessons
I've past all my test and I
know I'ma mess but I proved
I submitted

Sitting here wishin that I never listened
You take what you dish in
I'm drowning senses
I know what I'm missing
Refusing to get it
Influenced by menace
The darkness unhidden

Walk by faith, not by sight
Come take hand as we dance with the devil tonight
Carefully, you will see, oh don't you cry
As we dance with the devil tonight
You and me, gracefully, I'll hold you tight
As we dance with the devil tonight
I'm your soul, I'm your mind, I'll make you mine
As we dance with the devil tonight

Smoking to numb when I really look dumb
You look good in that tux
You know just what I want
It's like I'm hypnotized and decisions aren't mine
Yet I want to oblige and still stay by your side

No fleeing this feeling
My life has no meaning
My life source decreasing
Soul constantly screaming
My heart slowly beating
I feel so defeated
Don't know what I'm seeking
Just come find it with me

Walk by faith, not by sight
Come take my hand as we dance with the devil tonight
Carefully, you will see, oh don't you cry
As we dance with the devil tonight
All alone, I'm your home, you know your mine
As we dance with the devil tonight
Forever stained, made to stay, can't run away
When we dance with the devil tonight

ℬℙ𝒟

Don't know where to start, it's so much pain in my heart
It's like I'm broken to the core, don't
wanna be here anymore
Sitting crying on the floor, I know I'm damaging my world
I know I'm drowning in my hurt, I
know I wanna leave this earth
I'm beyond misunderstood, talk to family? Wish i could
If I could heal faster I would, I know
your tired of my mood
I just want the chance to move, I'm
beaten down black and blue
I don't wanna hurt you, splitting thinking got me hooked
BPD gotta hold on me
It won't set me free
Likes to see me bleed
Please come help me
So blind can't see
Where's my personality? Where is my normality?
Scared these meds won't work
I know I'm not enough
I know these placements shit dirt

I know I do too much to feel safe and heard
Please hear my words
To be just like you, no problems, no curse
Please just understand, I'm doing as much as I can
Didn't wanna go to school, all this
judgement stabbing wounds
I know I love what I do, no motivation couldn't do it
Getting punished for my failure, by
my parents and my razor
To myself I am a stranger, look in the mirror and I hate her
All around me I feel danger, tie the
rope and get to hanging
Imma blame it on my maker, I'm
just tired of looking crazy
I just wanna say I made it, prove to all I can take it
Get to the top n y'all gone hate it

Untitled

Born a orange flower, a little different than the rest
Nothing some extra support and attention can't fix
She's still tall, and bright, easily attracting bees
Thriving beautifully, authentically
Time passes, growth happens, and
the differences start stacking
"This flowers not normal! Why is this happening!?"
She's getting too difficult, there are other priorities
All the other flowers are growing so normally
Grab the chemicals, get a good fertilizer, do
the bare minimum and stabilize her
But why the chemicals? Where's the love?
Just gonna stabilize me assuming you know what's up???
You claim to know me, but idk myself
You covered me in fertilizer, fear engraved in my shell
Yea I was different, also no less or easy to love
Or was I not worth the extra effort?
Was I really too much?
Once vibrant and open, bright and charming
Now dull and closed in the shadows with no lighting
You can always learn to garden though, it's not much to it
Even going in not knowing what your doing
I know now in your heart you didn't want
this garden, so that part didn't matter
I got sun, water, and soil picture perfect on a platter
Why do the most for only one flower?
Especially one that's as messed up as ours
I've agreed with this before, allowing my light to dull
No longer using negativity as my fuel
This garden is toxic and I'm pulling my roots

Stoner Wannabe

I thought I was a stoner, but I'm really a runner
Rather face a blunt than the demons in my frontal
Couldn't stand being sober, too ashamed of myself
Let the weed dull me down and push away how I felt
When you hear about addiction you
think meth and cocaine
But it takes many forms, anything can trap your brain
Lying to myself, saying it's just for fun
Wake up like a junkie, can't function without some nugs
Saying I'll be productive after a few hits
Just to do nothing but sit and get my fix
Fiening so hard I'd justify stealing
Taking from a man who provides it willingly
All I have to do is ask but I'm impatient and greedy
I need to smoke now and get more
than what you'd give me
I need to dampen my light so I don't feel
embarrassed for being charm
I want my whole personality shoved in the dark
It's so draining not being charm, it
hurts knowing I ran from me
So I'm no longer running from my
feelings, no longer smoking weed
I just be charm and not a Stoner Wannabe

Grow

I feel like a flower trying to bloom in an ocean
Using all my leaves to grow just to see them floating
I say it's okay and I just need to fight, it's not
like i have resources to leave the tide
Drowning and choking but just watching it all happen
There's other flowers here keeping me trapped in
On the outside looking in these
flowers seem well bloomed
Even as heavy darkness loomed
I'll never see their petals nor how they seem so okay
But I'm my own flower longing to swim away
The shaking waters constantly running
Days are either all too rainy or all too sunny
I thought the water was calm and the waves peaceful
Everyone knows it's not, blatantly deceitful
I need my petals above water, out of the sea
I want my leaves back
I wanna be me
To stick my stem in soil, feel the breeze in the air
To release the turmoil and free my hair
Now it only feels like a dream and you
say I can't do that without money
What the hell does money have to do with my happiness?
It's nothing to a flower, fueling me with
discouragement, draining my power
Your beliefs aren't mine and you don't even respect that
So why are you still the cause of my setback?

My Biggest Lie

I don't like drugs
I never did
Curiosity didn't kill the cat
It was already killed
Yea it's intriguing, why not try it once?
Do it for the plot, get some stories stacked up
I tried, I loved it, holy shit i had weed
Secretly though, I just liked not being me
My ability to romanticize, glamorize, and lie
Had me convinced I'd be stoned til I die
You know "conceal don't feel, don't let them know"?
Well they knew because before the
mask all it did was show
If my tiger like arms wasn't enough, I
didn't know how else to speak up
Even if I did, I still got no love
So if they gave up, didn't really try,
why would anyone else?
Clearly I'm a handful, I see that, I'm myself
It's easier to be high out of my mind in my personal hell
It's weirdly comforting knowing I won't
be accepted coming out this shell
I dont't wanna be hurt again and not taken seriously
I don't feel safe and I don't know how to be
How do I feel like I'm not too much?

Regardless of my preference, how do I not do drugs?
Even if I stop weed there's still X and perkies
I'll go through the insomnia and a shit ton of hurling
Can't forget about liquor that I can
almost start getting on my own
Shot after shot, it gets easier on the throat
After all that shaking, crying, and false promises to god
You get up and do it all again like none of it happened
Well as long as I'm not myself I can pretend to be happy

Bipolar Bitch

I don't want to be here at all
But I love life and nothing is wrong
I'm tired of trying, I'm tired of being
I'm tired of the lack of positivity you're seeing
Who are you to judge when you don't even exist?
Who are you to judge when all you are is a bitch?
You're nothing but a fake, a false sense of hope
You're nothing but a nobody cracked up on dope
I give you someone real, I show you what's up
You just twist it around, and leave it in the dust
All you give is fear, you tell me the worst
I leave it in the dust so you don't feel hurt
You know that never works right? I always
come back around, I show you how you
really feel from the inside out
You're not always right and you're not always real,
it's not just what you give, all you are is fear
So what even are we? Why are we here?
Why can't we come together and both learn to steer?
I don't know and I don't care, y'all just
take control anytime and where

You decide if I'm up, you decide if I'm down
Everywhere I look, no personality is found
I don't know who I am unless it's one of you
Taking the wrong pills makes me so confused
I don't know if charm exist, I don't
know if she ever did too
I don't know how to not be everything I've been though
But I love life and nothing is wrong, I'll
come back soon and take back control

Bipolar Babe

I try to change, yet I stay the same
it won't go away, I can never escape
my disorderly ways so in love with the pain
I feel so insane
a bipolar babe
I don't know who I am, who I've been, or who I wanna be
Stuck in my head so constantly, not in touch with reality
I don't know where I stand or where
I'll land no personality
There's no one there's to comfort me,
my blades are here consistently
Not judging me but loving me
knowing how to tug on me
still here when it gets ugly
the only thing that hugs on me
that's there when I'm not functioning
the only thing that's love to me
it's everything I need
Cuz
I try to change, yet I stay the same
It won't go away, I can never escape
my disorderly ways too in love with the pain
I feel so insane
a bipolar babe

I know who I am, who I've been, and who I wanna be
patient #17
seven county beauty queen
drowning in my silent screams
a people pleasing fantasy
hiding all insanity while being what you want from me
picture perfect on the screen
I'm bleeding in my long sleeves
always It's exhausting
existing so invisibly
I know that you're not into me
I know that you're not listening
I know you're not just visiting
In love with my conditioning
I yearn for what I'm witnessing
It's constantly belittling
created my reality
negative and limiting
Cuz
I try to change, yet I stay the same
It won't go away, I can never escape
my disorderly ways so in love with the pain
I feel so insane
a bipolar babe

A Letter To Charm

You are kinda pissing me off but I know I should be nicer
You did what you did because you were none the wiser
I hate you still do the same things
I even hate that you changed
I changed for the better but you will never see it that way
You don't understand the path I unpaved
Duh I see it that's the fucking problem
What happens to drowning in drugs,
doing nothing and staying that way
You're ripping your life away and I can't unbreak the chain
I don't want to leave, you keep pushing me out,
I was good for you then why not now?
I know I'm sorry it hurts, I don't like it
either but I don't want us to die
We can make it I'll make you see it
But when you do that I'll be gone I won't
hold us back or keep us safe
More importantly, you just won't get in the way
But how do I know it's okay?
I'm a you I can trust, I'm the you you needed
And it doesn't have to be bye now
But I'm glad you can see it

Acknowledgements

Youtube is my world, people like MatPat, Markiplier, Wassabi Productions, Koala Puffs, and Macdizzle420 made me feel seen and accepted, provided laughter when there was none, and simply gave me something to live for and look forward too when I had nothing else. Wassabi Wednesdays was the only day of the week I looked forward to throughout my last few years at Wellington Elementary. Their first video got me into nightcore and that's when I learned I was "different". "That's white people music". It really hurt feeling like I wasn't not only allowed to like that kind of music but not be called black. I learned through koala puffs that it's okay to be weird, you can still be loved. I remember lowkey judging her myself for her sporadic behavior but I was really confused on how she could act so goofy around people and they still enjoy her. I also loved feeling like I had someone to smoke with. The longer I watched her the more I felt okay being odd. Along with that, Wassabi productions made 1, just 1 video of them playing Five Nights At Freddy's. After that I was in loveee. I needed to know the loreeee! So from there I stumbled upon Markiplier. I'll never forget my first impression of him, a deep, loud, soothing, voice that cusses a lot. I wasn't allowed to do either so it was comforting finding someone so okay being that way. I see cuss words as Patrick puts it best, "sentence enhancers" and it makes a difference when expressing yourself. I felt repressed not being able be loud and just say "FUCK!" But as we all know, Mark doesn't get into the lore, so, someway somehow I find MatPat. And omggg when I'm talking about seen, I was

SEEN! I was always told I'm thinking too deep about things and It's never as serious as I'm making it seem. I just need to "chill", essentially to "shut up". Seeing how much he "overthought", went about finding out the reasonings behind things, and how passionate he was lit up something different in me. It was like my intelligence was acknowledged and confirmed not just in the form of an A or Distinguished. The way he would get sooooo so deep into whatever he was figuring out and pay attention to the things most people look over filled me with so much warmth and excitement. I wasn't used to seeing someone be as elevated as I was about the lore behind things. Watching Markiplier play Fnaf for the past 11 years with MatPat breaking down the lore has been such a constant light in my life. Don't even get me started on the music, it's literally heaven sent. So one day in August I was watching a Macdizzle video where she opened up about her struggles with doomscrolling so she decided to take a social media break for a week. It hit hard because I knew how much I depended on YouTube to get me through the day, too scared and depressed to do anything else. One of the main things I took from that was how productive she became and that feeling of accomplishment through hard times. So I chose to do that the same day. With social media no longer holding me down I encouraged myself to get my ass out there and do whatever makes my heart warm. That same week I came across this poetry workshop + reading event on eventbrite that lit me up again and I knew I had to go. It was the best decision I've made in months. I would love to thank Ellan Hagan for truly inspiring me and proving to me that I can put myself out there and be the change I want to see. Thank you for giving me the experience I needed to spark that "YES!" energy. You were my sunshine in my storm that ignited a rainbow.